PRACTICAL *Art* SCHOOL

DRAWING WITH
PASTELS

DRAWING WITH
PASTELS

GERALD WOODS

LEOPARD

D R A W I N G   W I T H   P A S T E L S

CLB 4342

This edition published in 1997 by Leopard, a division of
Random House UK Ltd, Random House
20 Vauxhall Bridge Road, London SW1V2SA

Copyright © 1995 CLB International, Godalming, Surrey

ISBN 1 85170 557 0

This book was designed and created by The Bridgewater Book Company Ltd
and produced by CLB International
Designers Peter Bridgewater / Annie Moss
Editor Viv Croot
Managing Editor Anna Clarkson
Photographer Jeremy Thomas
Typesetter Vanesa Good / Kirsty Wall

Printed and bound in Spain

Contents

At-A-Glance Guide

7

Introduction

It is a curious fact that we owe the unique development of pastel technique to the failing eyesight of the painter Edgar Degas. As the constraints of fine brushwork gradually eluded him, Degas turned his attention to the broader and more direct technique of soft chalk pastels. He eventually found a way of using the medium with great fluency, accentuating and concealing at one and the same time the plastic movement of the human form in his prolific studies of dancers. In a sense, Degas liberated the medium by exploiting the cumulative strokes of raw pigment. In describing Degas' portrait of Durante, the critic J. K. Huysmans gave an illuminating insight into the artist's technique:

'The almost bright pink patches on the forehead, the green on the beard, the blue on the velvet of the sitter's collar; whilst the fingers are made up of yellow edged with bishop's violet. Near to, it consists of a hatching of colours which are hammered out and split up and appear to encroach one on the other; but at a few paces everything is in harmony and melts into the exact flesh tone.'

Degas' pastels bear the imprint of his supreme gift as a draughtsman, but those passages which are burnished and blended produce an effect which is virtually a form of painting. It is, however, the directness of the medium which makes it particularly appealing to those artists who work directly from observation – a broad range of colour and tone can be established quickly and the work completed in a single session.

To work confidently with pastels one needs to have some basic understanding of colour contrasts and harmony. When asked 'But how did you manage to get such vivid colour in those dancers? They are as brilliant as flowers', Degas responded by saying, 'With the neutral tone, *parbleu.*'

The first part of the book is devoted to materials and techniques, including basic exercises designed to give the beginner more control over the medium. Colour, composition and tone are explored in relation to the particular constraints of the medium. Mixed media techniques are included to demonstrate how the range of colour and texture can be extended. The particular problems of working in pastel directly from observation – translating what we see, depicting mood and atmosphere and sketchbook studies – are considered in relation to specific themes and subjects.

In the second part of the book, three artists have produced a series of ten projects, working in their own individual style, but using the same sources of reference. There is an introduction to each project, examining the specific problems posed by the diverse subjects. The development of the projects is revealed in step-by-step illustrations, offering a unique insight into the working methods of each artist. There follows a brief critique of the finished work, looking at salient points of achievement in terms of drawing, colour, composition and so on.

All art ultimately requires a physical act and none of the ideas propounded in this book will begin to make sense until that moment when, having opened your recently purchased box of pastels, your fingers become ingrained with pigment as you begin to construct the world you see around you, in your own terms.

MATERIALS
AND
TECHNIQUES

Choosing Pastels

Soft pastels are quite simply sticks of moulded pigment mixed to a binder to form a 'paste'. Generally, gum tragacanth is used as a binder but there are also a number of other equally suitable binding agents. The sticks are extremely fragile and are supported by an outer layer of tissue paper which can be peeled back as the work progresses.

One important advantage that pastels have over painting media such as oil and gouache is that, whereas paints can dry to either a lighter or darker tone, pastels do not undergo any such change.

The enormous colour range available in pastels is made possible by reducing the stronger primary, secondary and tertiary colours with a white base filler to produce an extensive sanicle of delicate tints. When selecting your own colour palette, there are a number of points worth considering. Think about the kind of subjects to which you are drawn – landscapes, portraits, flower studies, for instance, all require a basic range of colours, but you might need a number of neutral tints in addition to express light and shade, or your preferred subject may demand a dominant hue. Remember that almost every subtle nuance of colour in your drawing will require a separate stick of pastel. It sometimes happens that a carefully placed colour can provide a keynote to the entire work. The colour and tone of the paper support that you choose will also influence the degree of brightness and contrast in the finished work.

The characteristic crumbly texture of soft pastels produces very different marks to those made with coloured chalks or wax crayons. Used forcefully, a stick of soft pastel can be diminished rapidly, and the beginner might initially find them difficult to handle. The quality of soft pastels varies considerably; the less expensive ranges, for example, might be made from synthetic pigments and a high proportion of white filler.

Hard pastels contain a higher proportion of binder and are more tightly compressed. They produce a much sharper line and are used primarily for the initial structure when building up a pastel drawing. The pastels are sharpened either by breaking the stick, leaving a sharp point on each corner, or by wearing down one tip of the pastel on a pad of sandpaper. The pigment deposited from hard pastels is less

Soft pastels

Stiff brush

likely to be absorbed into the grain of the paper than soft pastel pigment and, as a consequence, is much easier to remove – preferably with a stiff painting brush.

Your initial palette might well consist of, say, six hard pastels – four primaries and a stick each of black and white – and 35 soft pastels, chosen individually rather than as a boxed set. Try to include a scale of warm and cool neutral tints in your selection and include a few special colours such as Carmine Red or Olive Green. Ideally, you will need to have a light, middle and dark tone of each colour which means that for a basic palette of 12 colours you will need 30 pastels. Manufacturers generally grade pastels according to the strength of each colour. A permanent deep red, for instance, might be produced as a pale tint in No. 1 grade and a more intense shade in No. 10 grade. Some manufacturers prefer to denote the amount of white filler used in reduction, expressed in percentage decimal points. Confronted by a huge range of colours in an art store, however, I tend to select by sight – or rather, the colours select me!

PASTEL PENCILS

Pastel pencils are used when finer detail is required, since they can be sharpened to a fine point. They have the advantage of being protected by the outer wood casing which helps to prevent breakage. If you are used to drawing with a pencil, you might be tempted to use them alone, not in conjunction with sticks of soft pastel. This would be a mistake, in my view, since you would never be able to experience the freedom of expression that comes from the broader application of coloured pigment.

OIL PASTELS

Oil pastels are a comparatively recent addition to pastel technique. The main difference is that they require an oil-based binder. With their consequent high grease content, the drawn strokes from oil pastels are less granular but more transparent than those made by soft chalk pastels. The colours are generally stronger, more intense and darker in tone. They should not be used in conjunction with chalk pastels because of their mutual antipathy. Once deposited on the paper support, oil pastels can be further diluted with white spirit to produce a coloured glaze effect.

Oil pastels

White spirit

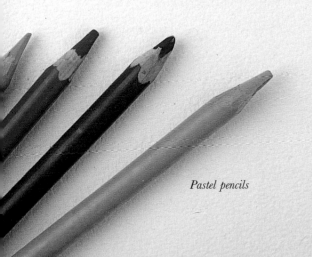

Pastel pencils

Making your own Pastels

14

Although one is spoilt for choice when it comes to purchasing pastels in an art store, the fact is they are quite simple to make at home – and much less expensive. The whole process of blending and binding pigment yourself can enhance your understanding of colour values. Another advantage of making your own pastels is that you can shape them individually – large or small, fat or thin, according to your own preference.

There are a number of recipes for binders; it is perfectly possible, for example, to make a rather brittle pastel using gum arabic alone as a binder. The gum should be mixed with distilled water in a proportion of 1:20. Cellulose-based wallpaper paste will also work as a binder. The best binder, however, is gum tragacanth, which has been in use since the Egyptians used it in their wall paintings. It is readily available in art supply shops.

Pastels stored in uncooked rice to prevent damage.

1 *In a glass or ceramic mixing bowl, add one measure of gum tragacanth to five parts distilled water. Add a few drops of beta naphthol with an eye-dropper, as a preservative. Because some pigments are likely to absorb more or less of the binding medium, this measurement can only be an approximation, so that your first attempt at making pastels will be subject to trial and error.*

2 *Pour some of the pure pigment onto a glass or marble mixing slab and add an equal quantity of white chalk. Mix the dry powders together thoroughly with a spatula and divide the mixture in half. Use one half to make the pastel and keep the remainder to reduce to paler tints of the same colour.*

3 *Now add the binder a few drops at a time and blend to a stiff paste using a wedge-shaped palette knife. (For finer results use a glass or stone muller for the grinding process). The consistency should be firm but not sticky. Scrape the mixture onto a sheet of blotting paper to drain off excess water.*

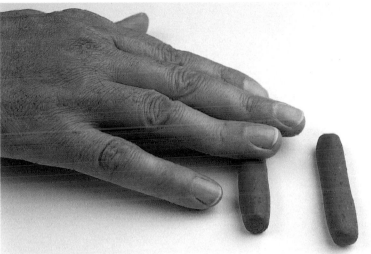

4 *Take a lump of the mixture and roll gently on to the slab using the length of the index finger. Be careful not to make the stick too thin. Place each moulded stick onto a drying tray lined with a paper towel and leave to dry for at least 48 hours.*

5 *I rather like the irregular shape of hand-finished pastels, but if you prefer a more uniform shape and size, you might consider making a simple mould. Write your own labels for the finished pastels indicating the colour and strength of the tint.*

LOOKING AFTER PASTELS

Pastels thrown together in a box tend to become dirty, as pigment dust transfers from one stick to another. Consequently, it becomes difficult to recognise the original colour without first removing an outer layer of dust. Most of the pastellists I know are also inveterate collectors of old cigar boxes, which are ideal for storing pastel fragments. Good-quality soft pastels are expensive, but with a little forethought and care, they can last a long time. Warm and cool hues might be stored in separate boxes, and special tints and colours in another box. Loose pieces of pastel can be stored and separated from each other, either by putting a layer of uncooked rice in the box, or by using corrugated paper to create separate compartments. Pastels must be stored in dry conditions; moisture will promote the formation of mould.

Surfaces and Supports

Pastels demand a paper which has a raised surface texture, or 'tooth'. Whereas watercolours, gouache and acrylics are absorbed into the paper itself, pastel stays on the surface. The action of drawing forces the pigment to be compacted into the minute hollows and ridges on the textured paper, an effect which is seen clearly under a magnifying glass.

Degas sometimes used tracing paper as support – mainly because he was able to place one sheet over another, continually correcting the drawing. These sheets were later glued to Bristol board. When using other papers, he would first soak them in turpentine so that the pastel pigment, when applied, would adhere more readily to the surface.

Apart from the texture of the paper surface, you also need to give some consideration to the colour and tone. Would your subject, for instance, benefit from a warm or cool base colour, or a pale or dark tone? Again, Degas often treated the base colour of the paper as an integral part of the subject he was drawing. As I write, I am looking at a reproduction of a pastel drawn by Degas of Ellen Andrée. On the base colour of green-grey, he has drawn the main outline of the figure in charcoal which is overlaid with just three pastel colours – Olive Green, white/pink and a rich aubergine. The total effect is of a colour harmony.

TONED PAPERS

Ingres, Canson and Fabriano papers are all suitable for pastels. Ingres paper is sometimes produced as a 'laid' paper, which means that the surface texture of close parallel lines is produced by the wire mesh of the mould. The range of colour and tone of these papers is extensive, but your choice will be determined to some extent by the subject. Light-toned papers, for example, are best suited to those subjects which demand a progression from mid to dark tones. Middle-toned papers are most popular with beginners since they tend to enhance the paler tints of pastel colour. The rich colour and texture of a paper, however, cannot detract from any weakness in the drawing itself. Dark-toned papers are difficult to use and are reserved mainly for certain subjects, such as interiors, where there might need to be greater contrast between light and dark tones. As a general rule, I would say

A selection of Ingres papers

Crushed pastel pigment

that the colour, tone and texture of the paper should not impose too much on the drawing itself.

There are some coloured papers which have been given a surface very similar to that of fine sandpaper. These are produced in a range of colours in pale and dark tones. I find that I am very sensitive to the tactile quality of paper, however, and although such papers are excellent technically, I dislike working with the kind of surface which produces a very mechanical looking drawn line. Large sheets of fine sandpaper can, of course, be given a base colour with gouache or acrylics.

TONING PAPER

Watercolour papers made from 100% cotton are sufficiently absorbent to allow an even tone to be laid on the surface. You can do this in a number of ways: for example, crushed pastel pigment can be taken up on a damp cloth and rubbed into the surface of the paper. Watercolour and gouache can also be diluted to produce a light or dark stain which can be brushed onto the paper. You may also like to experiment with other substances such as shellac or cold tea!

WHITE PAPER

If you prefer to work directly on to watercolour paper you will need to bear in mind the fact that pastel colours will appear to be slightly darker. If I am working with pastel on watercolour paper, I tend to combine it with charcoal as I find that this helps me to get the tonal balance right.

Tubes of gouache and watercolour

Cloth for rubbing pigment into the surface

CARDBOARD, MILLBOARD AND CARPET UNDERLAY

Henri de Toulouse-Lautrec (1864–1901) and Edouard Vuillard (1868–1940) both used a bisquit-coloured cardboard for pastels, gouache and even oils. The paper used for underlaying carpets, which is thick and often has an interesting colour and texture, is also very suitable for pastels. It often happens that when you are working on materials that have cost very little, you feel less inhibited about making mistakes and, as a consequence, the drawing is often livelier and less constrained.

Different Papers

Barcham Green
'Crisbrook' Handmade
paper (unsized)
300gsm/140lb. Soft-
sized or unsized hand-
made rag paper is
particularly receptive to
chalk pastels.

White Canson
Mi-teintes
190gsm/90lb. This is
an acid-free paper with
a soft, textured surface.
It is produced in a range
of tints and can be used
for pastels, crayons and
watercolours.

Grey Ingres pastel p
190gsm/90lb. This
fibrous paper is char
terised by the 'laid'
linear texture which
breaks up the stroke
a chalk pastel in an
interesting way.

Bockingford watercolour
paper, cold-pressed,
190gsm/90lb. This is
a robust, cold-pressed
watercolour paper that
is acid-free and can take
a lot of punishment.

Flocked pastel paper,
sand-coloured,
300gsm/140lb. The
soft 'tooth' of this paper
retains the crispness of
the stroke – but
corrections are more
difficult.

Canford paper
190gsm/90lb. This
strong cover paper has a
smooth surface and is
manufactured in a range
of 51 matt colours.

Additional Equipment

DRAWING BOARDS

If you intend working both in the studio and out of doors, then you will probably need two boards: a heavy, wooden commercial board and a lightweight board (plywood, hardboard or masonite) for sketching. Try to ensure that both boards are about 10cm/14in wider on all sides than the paper. It is advisable to use some sheets of old newsprint as padding between the paper and the board to produce a more tensile surface to work on and to prevent pastels breaking on an otherwise hard surface.

TABLES AND EASELS

Most pastellists prefer the sturdy support of a wooden table to an easel. There are exceptions of course – an easel is far more useful when doing life studies or portraits. If you prefer an easel, make sure that all the joints are tight, as a sudden knock or too much vibration when drawing can very easily displace the fine pigment at a critical stage.

PASTEL ERASERS

Kneadable erasers are particularly useful when working with pastels since, as the name suggests, they can be kneaded into any shape or point to enable the artists to lift out the surface pigment of any part of the drawing to be corrected. Never rub or burnish the surface of a pastel drawing – this will simply produce a greasy smudge and destroy the unique character of the chalk stroke.

Before using an eraser, brush away any loose particles of pigment with a hog's hair brush of the type used for oil painting. The same brush can also be used to make slight tonal adjustments before the drawing is finally fixed. Unwanted areas of pigment can also be gently scraped away with a flat blade. Make sure that the blade is absolutely flat against the surface of the paper.

Soft brush for blending

Emery boards

Scalpel

Kneadable eraser

Torchons

TORCHONS (PAPER STUMPS)

These can be used both for erasing the top layer of pigment and for blending pigments together. The paper stumps are made in different sizes, but you can just as easily make your own from sheets of tightly rolled blotting paper.

BLENDING BRUSHES

Several large, soft mop-haired blending brushes are useful, especially when working on a larger scale. Finer sable brushes can be used for small areas of the drawing where you need to soften the effect without removing the pigment.

SHARPENING PASTELS

Use an emery board containing parallel sheets of fine and coarse emery paper, or ordinary emery boards, as a base to sharpen pastels by rubbing the stick across the surface. Alternatively, shave the edge to a point with a scalpel or craft knife.

Fixing Techniques

Artists who work frequently in pastel tend to regard fixatives as a necessary evil. This is due in part to the fact that fixative does tend to spoil slightly the dry, fresh colour that distinguishes pastel from other media. There is a tendency for colour to darken as the pigment absorbs the viscous spray. The problem can be overcome to some extent by 'staggering' the process of spraying. A light spraying of fixative at each stage of the drawing will ensure that the pigment is stabilised without affecting too seriously the brilliance of the colour. This way, if there is any change in colour after the fixative has dried, it can be corrected before the next stage.

Excessive spraying is common and this, unfortunately, does the most damage to a pastel drawing, since the pigment is flattened or spread by the force of the spray into a paste-like consistency. It is better to under-spray than to saturate the paper. If you are using a fairly absorbent paper it will help if you also spray the drawing from the back.

For convenience, fixative is available in aerosol spray cans. Alternatively, the fixative can be atomised through a folding spray diffuser (available from art supply shops). This offers a greater degree of control since the flow is directed by blowing directly into the mouthpiece of the diffuser.

Cats are wise creatures – whenever I attempt to spray fixative on a drawing, my black cat departs with alacrity from the room! The fact is that the fumes are unpleasant and can be harmful to anyone with respiratory problems. Spraying should be carried out with plenty of ventilation.

SPRAYING PROCEDURE

Fix the drawing to a board or an easel or lay it flat. First of all make sure that the drawing is reasonably stable and that there are no loose particles of pigment. Keep the spray at least 300mm/12in from the surface and use a sweeping action to direct the spray back and forth across the drawing in a continuous movement to prevent the spray from becoming concentrated in any one area. Always test the spray on a sheet of scrap paper first to make sure that the nozzle is not clogged.

Using a mouth diffuser is an alternative to an aerosol spray.

Mouth diffuser

MAKING YOUR OWN FIXATIVE

There are numerous recipes for making fixative – the most suitable for pastel is based on casein which is a glue derived from milk. Hilaire Hiler, author of the standard work *Notes on The Technique of Painting*, recommends the following receipt: Mix 20g/^{3}/$_4$oz of casein with an alkaline solution of 4g/^{1}/$_6$oz borax and enough distilled water to make a paste. After a few hours this becomes a syrupy mixture which should be thinned with 1l/1^3/$_4$pt of water. Add 600ml/1pt of pure grain alcohol and, after the solution has clarified, it can be stored in an airtight bottle ready for use. (Ammonia may be substituted for borax.) Apply home-made fixative with a spray diffuser.

A basic non-toxic fixative which is fairly reliable is skimmed milk; caseinogen is the soluble form of casein as it occurs in milk.

The aerosol is held firmly and used with a sweeping action at a distance of approximately 28cm/12in.

If you decide against fixing your pastels then you should seal them behind glass in a frame. Make sure that you clean the glass of the frame with a damp cloth to avoid static electricity build-up which would attract pigment particles to the underside of the glass.

Basic Strokes

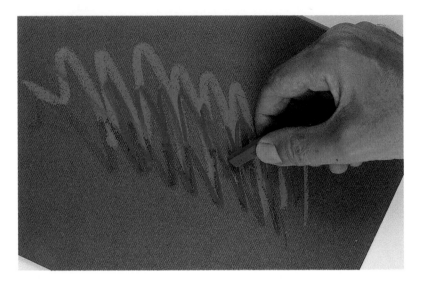

Before I start work I sometimes like to stroll down to the seashore to see what has been washed up by the morning tide. Quite often, I come across a web of different coloured fishing nets caught up on the rock. In a way, this reminded me how, in pastel drawing, one builds up colour with a web of cumulative drawn strokes, rather than by applying it in solid areas. Look, for example, at a Degas study of a nude bathing, and you will see how he seemingly carves out the form with vigorous intersecting strokes of pastel. Before you can draw with conviction, you will need to gain confidence in handling pastels so that the marks you make have the recognisable quality of being your own. If you happened to have bought a new box of pastels, take one stick from the box and break it in half. Then, pick up a broken fragment and begin to make arcs, spirals, thin lines and thick lines, with the kind of flowing gesture that comes from a supple writer. This kind of exploratory mark-making will enable you to gain the kind of control needed for more applied studies.

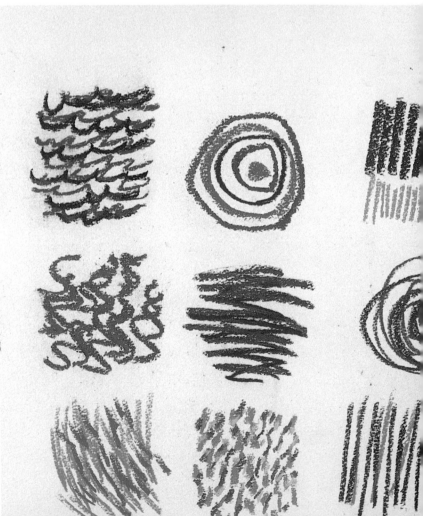

ABOVE *Practising a basic, direct stroke with chalk pastels on a dark-toned Ingres paper.*

Notice how the grain of the paper influences the quality of the line.

TOP RIGHT *Further experimenting, this time with three tones of one colour on a dark paper.*

The type of paper used will, in part, determine the granular quality of the stroke. On a smooth paper, for instance, the pastel stroke will be more dense. On a rough paper, the stroke will be broken into a halftone by the 'tooth'. A laid paper will break the colour with a series of fine, white parallel lines.

Try drawing on different papers with hard and soft pastels. Begin with a single colour, then try to build up webs of colour in two or three layers of broad cross-hatchings. When using the cross-hatching technique vary the space between lines. The closer the lines are together, the darker the tone will be. Try also interweaving complementary or discordant colours, or colours of the same hue, on light- and dark-toned papers. You will begin to see how colours blend optically as each hue, while retaining its own identity, also appears to blend with other colours in close juxta-

position. Colour produced in this way is more kinetic than flat areas of colour - which is why Degas' figure studies always seem to be in movement.

Hard pastels will generally produce better results when using this technique, especially when used on an HP drawing paper.

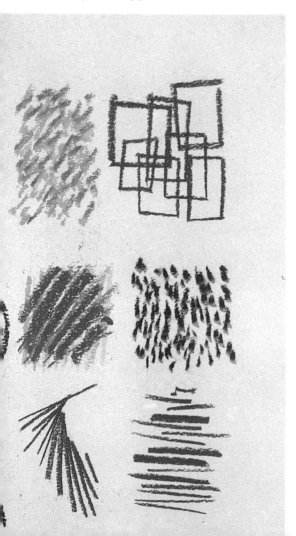

TOP RIGHT *A lighter tone of orange is hatched over the red producing an optical blending of the two colours.*

RIGHT *A cobalt blue is hatched over the red and orange creating the effect of movement.*

LEFT *Drawing random calligraphic squiggles is a good way to loosen up so that your drawing action is less stilted.*

Building up Solid Colour

Most pastel drawings combine the kind of linear strokes we have already practised with solid or semi-opaque areas of pure and blended colour. To produce a large area of colour it is best to use the length of the pastel laid flat on the surface of the paper. To create a continuous tone, the pastel is literally dragged over the surface, depositing a layer of colour that is broken only by the texture of the paper. Further layers can be added by applying more pressure until the right tone has been established in relation to the rest of the drawing. Again, experiment with hard and soft pastels and different papers in order to discover which combination suits your own intentions.

Without proper control pastels can be twisted and turned on paper to produce a rather mechanical pattern; resist, if you can, the temptation to incorporate any slick marks into your drawing. Always try to make the medium work in the service of an idea.

2 *A layer of solid red applied over the ultramarine intensifies the tone as the two colours are blended together.*

1 *Using the length of a stick of ultramarine chalk pastel to produce a continuous tone which is broken only by the grain of the paper.*

3 *A more intense blending of colour is achieved by applying more pressure – the first two colours are almost cancelled out by a layer of Burnt Sienna.*

ABOVE *Illustration to a story by
Cecilia Hunkeler. The two old ladies
in traditional Breton costume are
drawn in solid layers of oil pastel
working directly onto a double-page
spread of a French newspaper.*

Blending, Merging and Feathering

28

One of the most attractive features of the medium of pastel drawing is that colours can be blended and fused together easily to produce the most beautiful gradations. Pastel colours, once put down, retain their luminosity and do not sink like other media. In certain conditions, the light is refracted by the surface of the pigment so that the drawing appears to stand in relief. Adjacent colours can be blended together with your fingertip, torchons, brushes, soft cloth or tissue. Additionally, you can moisten the pigment by steaming it – as Degas did – before blending.

Of course, the blending of colours should only be done as an integral part of the overall drawing. In a landscape drawing, for example, you might want to suggest recession and aerial perspective by blending colours in the middle-distance and sky. When working on a still life, you might need to blend the colour to suggest the form of curved or rounded objects. There are few occasions when you would use blended colour alone – a seascape,

LEFT *A drawing of a life model using a feathering technique to suggest the fleeting quality of the light.*

LEFT *Using a soft brush to blend colour in a part of the drawing where the pigment has become too heavy.*

RIGHT *Blending colour by gently burnishing with a finger – this is the most direct way of fusing colours together.*

LEFT *A torchon can be used for blending local areas of colour on a large drawing, especially in portraiture.*

perhaps, or a sky study – but, generally, blended colour should be harnessed in some way by broken linear strokes.

MERGING

The effect of three-dimensional modelling is achieved by blending colours from a light tone to a mid-tone and then towards a dark tone in relation to the source of light. The eye responds to a variety of soft and hard forms, and in the best pastel drawings there is a balance between softly blended colour, hard and soft edges, and a descriptive line which pulls everything together. The degree to which the linear element is either overstated or understated is determined by the nature of the subject. If, for instance, you wanted to say something about the intensity of light in a landscape seen at mid-day, you might ruin the whole effect if you allow for too much vigorous linear description.

Blending is a form of mixing colour on the surface, and while this might produce interesting results with two or three colours, the technique becomes unworkable if too many colours are used; the colour becomes dirty and the paper will no longer retain the pigment.

For large areas of colour – the sea, sky or a field, foreground or background – it is best to use a finger or a soft rag to gently merge one colour into another. For figure studies, where the drawing is prominent, I would tend to use a soft brush so that, as the colours merge, part of the underlying contours is revealed. A torchon is used for blending colour in small areas – when modelling the features of a portrait, for instance, or the intricate shapes of a flower study.

FEATHERING

Feathering colour simply means drawing strokes rapidly, applying very little pressure. It is a technique that can be used to relieve the monotony of a flat, underlying tone or to bring an overall unity to a drawing when the various disparate elements don't seem to jell together. Essentially, it is a means of modifying tones that are too light or dark. An area of a drawing that is too cool in tone, for example, might be feathered with a tint of red to correct the balance.

Drawing with Pastel Pencils

Pastels in pencil form are a convenient means of extending the range of the medium. Strips of compressed pigment 5mm/^{1}/$_5$in wide are inserted into standard 8mm/^{1}/$_4$in diameter barrels. They are produced in an extensive range of colours and can be sharpened like ordinary soft pencils.

The character of the stroke produced by a pastel pencil, however, is more acute than that of conventional sticks of hard and soft pastels. Nevertheless, you might find the pencil form of pastel easier to control and, as a result, your drawing might become freer and more lucid.

Ideally, pastel pencils are best used in conjunction with hard and soft pastels. I would tend to use them when drawing rapidly from

observation – for figure drawing, portraits and sketchbook notations. They are particularly useful when trying to register architectural detail or any complexity of form and structure.

*Pastel pencils are useful
for making rapid sketches
on location – circus girl
(INSET) and Mount Rigi
on Lake Lucerne,
Switzerland (LEFT).*

Different Coloured Grounds

34

The French colour theorist Michel-Eugène Chevreul (1786–1889), suggested that the close proximity of grey causes colour to gain in brilliance. Because pastels are opaque and retain their brilliance, the use of a mid-toned pastel paper tends to induce an overall harmony and to enrich darker tones. By working directly onto a mid-grey paper, therefore, you will be better able to evaluate the tonal unity of the drawing.

If you are drawing in pastel onto a white or pale-tinted paper, the colour initially looks brilliant. When all the colours are blocked in, however, you are forced to assess colours in relation to one another, rather than in relation to the white ground. This can make tonal evaluation difficult, and when pastel drawings fail it often has more to do with the tone than the colour. The constant working and reworking of pastel on white paper can in itself create a tone, as the pigment is pushed around on the surface. For this reason, some artists like to use charcoal in combination with pastels when working on a white ground because the softer gradation of the charcoal pigment influences the tone of the pastels.

❶ *An Indian Red oil paint diluted with a spike of lavender oil is rubbed into the surface of watercolour paper to produce a base tint. The tone can be even or varied according to the tonal strength of the drawing you intend to lay on top.*

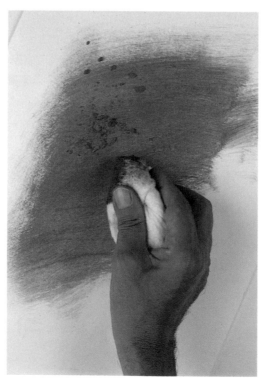

❷ *The residue of pigment collecting at the bottom of your pastel box can be used to create a base tint by forcing the grains into the surface of an unsized paper with a soft rag.*

❸ *Gouache produces an ideal ground for pastel drawings since it is a water-soluble paint made from coloured pigments and white filler which produces a matt, chalky base that readily accepts chalk pastels.*

BELOW *This life study is enhanced by the warm tone of the paper.*

RIGHT *A colour exercise using chalk pastels on soft, hand-made plant papers. Notice how the dark-toned paper lifts the colour values.*

USING DARK-TONED PAPER

The experience of working on a dark-toned paper can be quite rewarding, insofar as it will enable you to gain a better understanding of tonal values by having to reverse the normal procedure of working from light to dark. The progression from the near black of the paper towards lighter tones and colours concentrates the mind on the essential elements of the composition. If, for example, I happened to be drawing the interior of a room on a dark-toned paper, I would begin by breaking everything down into simple, abstract elements. The basic shapes of doors, floor and wall spaces, windows and so on, can be registered in terms of simple blocks of interlocking colour. Working in this way, the tonal progression can be worked out in simple steps. Try drawing on a dark-toned paper in circumstances where you would not normally choose to do so – you might surprise even yourself!

Colour

THE THEORY OF COLOUR

Colour theory is really a convenient way of organising and codifying colour into divisions based on the spectrum. The difficulty lies in relating one's intimately subjective experience to the objective principles of colour theory. Nevertheless, a basic knowledge of these principles can help to reinforce our own intuitive values. What is helpful is to learn how colours behave in relation to each other.

Sir Isaac Newton (1642–1727) demonstrated that although sunlight, or white light, is uncoloured, it is made up of seven coloured rays: red, orange, yellow, green, blue, indigo and violet. We see colour in objects that reflect and absorb these rays to a greater or lesser extent. The colour wheel is really a basic illustration of the spectrum.

Yellow, red and blue are the primary colours from which, theoretically, all other colours are made. Secondary colours (green, orange, purple) are produced by mixing any two of the primaries. Tertiary colours result from mixing a primary colour and a secondary colour together. In the manufacture of pastels, it is the addition of white which further extends the range of colour by breaking down the strength of the primary, secondary and tertiary colours into subtle gradations of tints.

Complementary colours refer simply to the 'complement' of each colour in its opposite on the colour wheel – thus red is the complement of green. When complementary colours are mixed together they cancel each other out.

If you look at the numerous colours and tints in a set of pastels you will see that the colours based on red/yellow/orange and the earth colours are warm in relation to those based on blue/green/violet, which are cool. The brighter reds, yellow and orange are characteristic of such basic life forces as the sun and of fire, whereas we find blues in the shadows of snow in a sunlit landscape. Warmer colours appear to advance and cooler colours recede when placed next to warmer hues. There are, of course, varying degrees of temperature within each colour category. A vermilion is warmer, for instance, than a magenta red.

Degas was a superb intuitive colourist and yet he claimed not to be preoccupied with colour. He once said that he would probably have stuck to black and white if the world had not clamoured for more and yet more of his vivid pastels.

Whenever I see a box containing dozens of chalk pastels, I always feel that the colours themselves suggest ideas. I can imagine grouping certain colours together to help me to give expression to unresolved or unformed images. And while there are so many tints and full colours to choose from, it is surprising just how much one can say with just a few carefully selected colours.

We come to an understanding of colour in different ways; some people approach the subject from the particular rules of colour theory, others rely entirely on intuition and intense observation. One can also learn a great deal from simply studying the work of artists who are known to be great colourists. There is, however, a danger in seeing the work entirely in the form of reproductions in art books – apart from the reduction in scale, the standard four-colour printing process rarely gets the balance right in relation to the original.

COLOUR HARMONY

There are essentially two ways of achieving colour harmony. First, by colour unity – using colours which are all to be found on one side of the colour circle. A landscape scene, for example, might be rendered in a range of ochres, warm yellow and burnt umber to produce a sombre harmony. The second way of creating harmony is by contrast, using carefully balanced tones of warm and cool colours. Joseph Mallord William Turner (1775–1851), for instance, used often to compose his paintings in assiduously modulated colours of yellow/ochre towards blue/violet.

LIGHT AND LOCAL COLOUR

The mixing and blending of colour is usually done in an interpretive way, based on observation of how an object appears under certain conditions of light. The 'local' colour of an object refers to the actual colour, rather than the colour perceived when that same object is illuminated by strong light or immersed in shadow. Let us suppose, for example, that you were to paint two wooden cubes Cadmium Red. Then, that you placed one of the cubes in bright sunlight and the other in shadow. The 'local' colour of both cubes would be the same, but the perceived colour value would be different.

It is easy to be certain about the 'local' colour of objects that are familiar – that we can touch or hold – but what is the 'local' colour of a mountain? We know that Paul Cézanne painted a series of studies of Mont Sainte-Victoire in Provence from a distance under different conditions of light. He was therefore concerned not with local colour, but with producing a summation of his experience, which he represented by using an interaction of warm and cool colour values.

If all of this sounds slightly confusing, there is no need for despair. You will find that your colour sense increases with practice. Colour is not something we see, but a way of seeing, and the way that we perceive colour is conditioned by our past and present experience.

ABOVE *A loosely stated colour circle drawn with chalk pastels: a great number of graded tints can be produced from each base colour.*

Tone

Colour should not be thought of as being a separate entity from tone; every colour has a tone. For instance, Prussian Blue and Burnt Umber are opposites in terms of colour, but both have approximately the same tone. Tones are produced by the quality and intensity of the light that is reflected from an object. Again, we need to be able to distinguish between the 'local' tone, and the way that a tone is modified by the quality of light which falls on any object. A house seen in sunlight from a distance will appear to us as a solid, three-dimensional object by virtue of the fact that the plane turned towards the source of light will be lighter in tone than those elevations which are turned away from the light. On a dull or a misty day, all such distinctions of tone would be levelled out or lost.

All pastel drawings need to have a tonal scheme; it is difficult to employ strong colours *and* strongly distinctive tones together. In the main, it is a question of balancing the strength of the colour against the strength of the tone. Many artists use colours which are close in tone; Vuillard, for example, used very subtle variations of tone in his distemper paintings and pastels. Pastel tints are close in tone and the fact that one can achieve such delicate variations in both colour and tone is part of the charm of the medium.

The mechanical tones of the photographic print have in part conditioned the way artists tend to use tone in terms of clearly defined stepped gradations. I believe that you need to look harder to uncover those barely perceptible changes of colour and tone which cannot be registered on photographic film. In the best tonal studies, detail is sacrificed in order to place more emphasis on the atmospheric and spatial dimensions of the subject.

THREE-TONE TECHNIQUE

As an exercise in tonal control, select three pastels of the same hue in a pale, mid and dark tone. Then, choose an object from your kitchen – a bowl, jug or coffee pot perhaps – and try rendering both the object and background using only the three tones. Begin with the palest tone; not just as a background colour, but also as an underlying tone for the other colours. Use the mid-tone to express modelling and the darkest tone to produce the contrast.

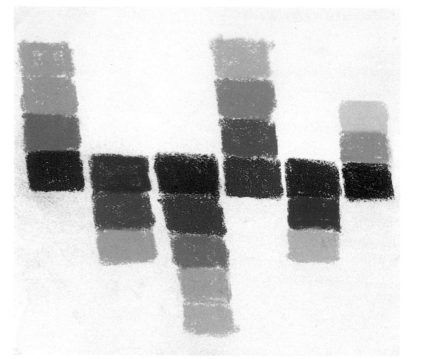

ABOVE *Gradations of colour drawn on a tonal scale. This simple exercise can help your understanding of the variety of tones that can be produced with pastels.*

LEFT *A portrait drawing using three tones: pale Naples yellow, olive green (tint) and raw umber. Greater tonal unity is achieved by using just a few closely related colours.*

ABOVE *Church at Tarring Neville, East Sussex, England. This tonal study employs warm and cool hues of chalk pastels overworked on to a base of watercolour washes.*

Space, Depth and Perspective

From the moment that I make my first mark on paper, I am beginning to establish a spatial dimension between that mark and the surface area of the paper itself. Then, as I begin to place patches of colour side by side, the varying colour and tone of each plane will suggest depth and recession. Some artists, for example, begin a pastel drawing by laying down large masses of broadly stated colour in order to establish right away the illusion of three-dimensional space. But the actual placement of those masses is of critical importance to the success of the drawing. Detail is of little consequence at this stage – if the basic spatial plan is unsat-

isfactory, then no amount of intricate topographical flourish can save it. We use colour and tone to control space. Colour advances and recedes and suggests in a symbolic way the sense of depth and recession in a drawing or painting.

Begin with a subject which can be broken down into simple shapes – a landscape perhaps, or an interior. Make a number of diminutive pencil sketches to establish the essential design of the subject in order to clarify, in your own mind, the way that planes are separated from one another in space.

LEFT *Still life – Three apples are carefully placed on a table-top in relation to each other and to the wooden boxes and blocks. This is a useful exercise, not only in terms of perspective, but also in visual judgement and composition.*

RIGHT *Landscape, Spain. Aerial perspective is suggested in a very subtle way in this drawing: the artist has worked on a mid-toned paper which unifies tones from the palest pink of the distant mountains to the rich umbers of the scrubland in the foreground.*

AERIAL PERSPECTIVE

We can also create a sense of space in landscape by considering the effects of aerial perspective. The pellucid veils of atmosphere (particularly in the northern hemisphere) reduce tones and make colours become cooler. For instance, you will have noticed how distant hills and mountains sometimes take on a tint of blue. The darkest objects in the foreground lead the eye towards the middle distance and on to the palest tones on the horizon.

Try to avoid thinking of aerial perspective as a formula or visual cliché – be selective and hint at the impalpability of changing light values, rather than recording too much detail. In his *Leaves from a Notebook*, Thomas Aldrich says 'I like to have things suggested rather than told in full. When every detail is given, the mind rests satisfied, and the imagination loses the desire to use its own wings'.

This, in my view, is what drawing in pastel is mainly about. It is a medium that lends itself to the recording of those incidents in everyday life which are transitory – a landscape briefly illuminated by the sun, figures in movement or informally posed.

Composition

> "
> *Even in front of nature, one must compose.*
> "
>
> Edgar Degas

Degas was acutely aware of the way that pictorial space need-ed to be organised in a logical way, even though his pastel drawings appear to be informal and entirely spontaneous. 'I assure you', he said, 'no art was ever less spontaneous than mine.'

His original approach to composition was influenced by the unconventional – to western eyes – compositions of Japanese prints, and by the photographic 'snapshot'. This led him to view his subjects from unexpected viewpoints and angles.

We can define composition as the logical disposition of the ele-ments in a drawing or painting. This is not to suggest that every-thing we draw or paint must be subjected to some kind of pre-ordained plan. We sometimes unconsciously put things down in a particular part of a drawing, simply because it seems right to do so. Again, we should pay attention to the master pastellist, Degas, who said that a picture is an original combination of lines and tones which make themselves felt.

The way that a picture is composed, therefore, might depend on exactly what our intentions are in relation to the subject. If, for example, I wanted to evoke the essential mood of a low-lying landscape in Holland, I would probably place the horizon line fairly low in my composition, with two thirds or more of the pic-torial space devoted to the sky. ·

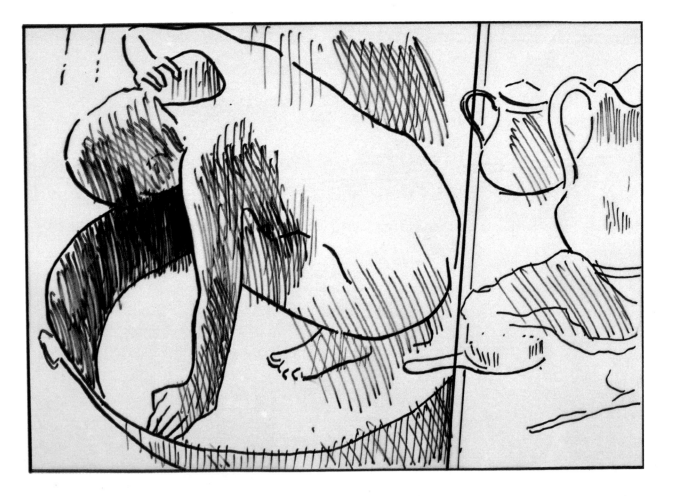

RIGHT *Compositional analysis of the pastel drawing by Degas, known as 'The Tub' (1886). The strong diagonal line on the right of the figure corresponds to the Golden Section.*

The whole process of composing a picture can begin long before you even start to draw. It is difficult to say why one place should command more interest than another, but I believe it has something to do with the particular relationship of parts; the way that in a landscape, for instance, all the elements – hills, trees, rivers and synthetic artefacts – are disposed. Then you begin to try to visualise how you might bring these disparate elements together in a drawing or painting. One advantage that the artist has over the photographer is that he or she can leave out unwanted detail and even move a tree, a building or any other element to produce a more satisfactory composition.

We must begin by relating the composition to the dimensions of the paper we are working on. Scale is an important factor – things are never isolated, but are relative. Degas produced two pastels with the title, 'The Tub'. In both drawings, the circular form of the metal tub is critically placed to act as a foil to the figure itself. The drawings are composed in such a way that every element counts – whether it's a hairbrush, jug or the edge of a chair. Nothing is allowed to distract from the essential relationship of the figure and the tub.

THE GOLDEN SECTION

The division of space known as the Golden Section is the best known device for dividing the picture plane aesthetically. It is based on the idea that the proportion of the smaller to the larger is the same as the larger to the whole. An easy way of finding the Golden Section of any given rectangle is to take a sheet of paper of the size you are working on, and fold it in half three times in succession. Do this for both the length and breadth of the paper. The folds will divide the paper into eight equal parts, from which a 3:5 ratio can be determined. Alternative ratios might be 2:3, 5:8 or 8:13. This device works best in compositions where one needs to draw attention to a single vertical element – a standing figure, a tree or even a telegraph pole.

Yet, if we accept what Degas said about combining lines and tones which make themselves felt, we must also consider contrast, light and tone, movement and the relationship between all these things. This may sound a tall order when all you want to

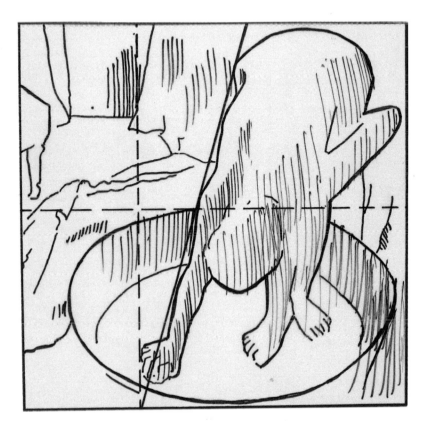

ABOVE *Compositional analysis of a second drawing by Degas, also known as 'The Tub', and produced in the same year.*

Notice the strongly diagonal accent of the pose and the way that the circular tub fits perfectly into the lower half of the composition.

do is get on with drawing the scene in front of you, but do try to get into the habit of being more selective. If it helps, make a simple framing device by cutting a square or rectangle from a piece of black card. Use it to frame the image to emphasise what you want. When you are seated in front of your subject, ask yourself what particular qualities about the subject interest you most. Then, try to compose your drawing in such a way that you draw attention to those qualities.

Translating what we See

...he who can interpret what has been seen is a greater prophet than he who has simply seen it.

St Augustine (AD 354–430)

We see what we expect to see, and what we expect to see is all too often conditioned by the way that other artists have interpreted various subjects before us. Although, for instance, I have made frequent references to Degas in this book – because he is an artist I happen to admire – I would not wish to emulate his style in any way, nor would I be particularly interested in his choice of subject matter. We must try to discover the world in our own terms, and be able to translate what we have seen through our chosen medium, without being affected too much by what other artists have done. We need to find a way of communicating our discoveries in a very personal way. The so called 'prim-

itive' painter Alfred Wallis (1855–1942) who, in his old age, painted sailing ships and Cornish harbours onto scraps of wood and cardboard, worked essentially from memory (of his days at sea) and imagination to convey images which are far more telling than those produced by 'trained' nautical painters who invested the same subject with densely packed incident and detail.

Nobody should have to tell you what to draw or paint; you need to be interested and excited by a subject for your own reasons. You might find it necessary to heighten certain colour contrasts, or exaggerate the scale of things, in order to make a particular point about the subject you are drawing. The degree of detail or finish invested in any drawing is dependent on just how much information you need to express to enable others to follow what you are trying to say. It is not necessary, for example, to draw every leaf on an olive tree for others to identify what species of tree it is. The artist should be judged by what he or she actually does with his subjects, not by what the subjects are.

LEFT *Spanish landscape. This is a good example of the way that the quality of light can be translated convincingly with just a few chalk pastel colours.*

You may find that you are excited by a particular subject not because you are actually interested in its intrinsic value, but because it allows you to explore values which are independent of the subject. For example, it would be possible for someone to produce an interesting pastel drawing of, say, a frying pan, a saucepan and a jug, without being interested in those objects *per se*, or attaching any meaning to them.

ABOVE *A rough pastel transcription from Poussin's painting 'Summer'. The purpose of this exercise is not to produce a copy, as such, but to interpret the main forms and colour relationships in a different medium from the original.*

Depicting Mood and Atmosphere

52

> *See this layered sandstone among the short mountain grass. Place your right hand on it, palm downward. See where the sun rises and where it stands at noon. Direct your middle finger midway between them. Spread your fingers, not widely. You now hold this place in your hand.*
>
> from *Black Mountain* by Raymond Williams

The work of certain writers, painters, poets, photographers and even musicians is often inextricably linked with a particular place or region. By close association you learn to uncover the spirit of a place, and to be cognisant of different levels of feeling. Turner's paintings varied dramatically in mood and atmosphere; from storms at sea and over the Alps, to the calm and brilliant scenes of the Venice lagoon, or hazy views of English castles seen at sunrise.

What do we mean when we say that a drawing or painting is atmospheric? 'Atmosphere' contains a duality of meaning; the particle-laden body whose transparency is dependent on variable atmospheric pressure, and the pervading mood of a place which in turn evokes certain feelings and emotions. Additionally, the mood and atmosphere of the work might also be dependent on the state of mind of the person producing it. Whereas I might depict a fishing harbour as a scene which reflects a kind of tranquil sadness, another artist might view the same scene in a more joyful and exuberant frame of mind.

We use colour by association to suggest mood, sometimes contrasting bright complementary colours with more sombre hues, or cooler colours to express quietude. One must be cautious, however, in confining colour values to such convenient categories.

ATMOSPHERE AND LANDSCAPE

When drawing a landscape or an architectural subject, we sometimes need to be patient, waiting for that time of day when the conditions of light will enhance the mood and atmosphere of the subject. Mountainous regions, for instance, are best seen in mist or after rain, when distances are difficult to define and contours less sharp. It might be necessary to rise at first light or wait until dusk to heighten the drama of the subject. In attempting to evoke the atmosphere of a place, you need to be more attentive to the influence of light than to the representation of detail. Light waves are conditioned by the way that they react to various substances – water, mist, cloud, stone and so on. Even under direct sunlight, the actual intensity of the light varies considerably from one part of the landscape to another. At sunset or sunrise there is a scattering of light caused by the molecules of air and by the presence of dust and moisture in the atmosphere. And when the sun is overhead at midday the light waves have a shorter distance to travel than at dusk or early morning.

RIGHT *Shop fronts in the Rue de la Ste Catherine, Dieppe, France. An intimate study in winter of this small square which has changed little since it was painted by Walter Sickert in 1900.*

INTERIOR MOODS

When working on interior subjects one can work with the available light source from doors and windows, or under artificial light, which can be controlled to some extent. Vuillard produced his most atmospheric pastels in the intimate surroundings of his own home. Start, then, with those subjects you know and love best and remember, although this may sound a truism, you are more likely to be aware of the mood and atmosphere of your own surroundings than you would be in unfamiliar territory.

LEFT *The mood of this drawing is largely determined by the low level of the available light source from the window.*

RIGHT *Spanish landscape. A study of the roof tops in a white village seen towards dusk, a time when contrasts are softer and colours more muted.*

Sketchbook Notations

54 John Constable (1776–1837) always carried a pocket sketchbook with him on his forays into the countryside. He used a sketchbook for what he called his 'hasty memorandums' – page after page was filled with diminutive studies in pencil of trees, skies, hedgerows, farm labourers and the effects of light and shadow on the landscape.

We use a sketchbook as a kind of visual diary to make personal notations of things seen, which need not be meaningful to anyone else. Pastel is an ideal medium for working in sketchbooks; no brushes, water or unwieldy equipment is required, only fixative, perhaps, or tissue between pages to prevent smudging. I prefer a spiral-bound sketchbook with assorted colours of Ingres paper. Sketchbooks made up from watercolour paper are also suitable. You can of course make up your own sketchbook using a variety of papers – I sometimes use a very thin Japanese paper, especially if I am combining charcoal with pastel. I have also seen some very beautiful pastel drawings in France that were produced on newspaper.

A sketchbook sets you free from the formal constraints of trying to produce a 'finished' pastel drawing. You should use it to take risks and to push the medium to extremes. In other words, don't be precious about it – use your sketchbook as a useful working tool. It sometimes happens that an artist's best work is to be found in his or her sketchbooks. This has something to do with the fact that all the freshness and conviction of the initial study is lost when it becomes formalised on canvas or paper. The difficulty in using sketchbook studies as reference for work produced on a larger scale in the studio is to maintain the spontaneity of the original study.

LEFT *Tree forms. A sketchbook study in charcoal.*

ABOVE *Pastel and charcoal sketches from the sketchbooks of Sophie Mason and Helen Armstrong.*

THE
PROJECTS

Artist • Sophie Mason

❶ *A Raw Sienna pastel is used to mark out the main shapes of the still life, particularly in relation to the horizon line of the table.*

❷ *Cadmium Yellow and Cadmium Orange are roughly scumbled into the foreground with a suggestion of the pattern on the tablecloth.*

❸ *Cadmium Red is used for the melon, peaches and plums to give body to the main shapes in the arrangement and to provide contrast to the background. The flowers in the background are roughed in with Cadmium Orange.*

| CADMIUM YELLOW | CADMIUM ORANGE | YELLOW OCHRE | RAW SIENNA | PERMANENT RED LIGHT | CRIMSON | PALE OLIVE GREEN | DARK OLIVE GREEN | MID GREY | BURNT UMBER | 6B PENCIL |

4 *Burnt Umber is applied to the skin of the melon and the background is darkened with Raw Umber.*

5 *Raw Umber and Burnt Umber are used to strengthen the background tone and to provide more definition to the flowers. Permanent red and light red are blended onto the peaches, melon and plums. The outer shape of the melon and plate is more carefully defined using graphite pencil and Burnt Umber.*

6 *Dark olive and pale olive are added to the background foliage to bring forward the shapes of leaves and to relate the background to the foreground. More grey is added to the plate. Greater definition is given to the flowers with Raw Umber and black pencil. Colour reflected from the fruit is added to shadows using Cadmium Yellow and Yellow Ochre.*

Still life · *Critique*

Drawing works well
in terms of colour
and tone

Good basic design
in the way that
shapes relate to
each other

SOPHIE One senses that the artist enjoyed working with the brilliant colours demanded by this subject. The drawing works well in terms of colour and tone and in the rich variety of marks made with chalk pastels. The artist has consciously avoided trying to make the drawing too illusionistic in terms of representing everything in three dimensions, preferring related shapes and interactive colour.

CECILIA The intensity of the colour and the range of textures – from smooth to coarse-grained fruit skins – has been dealt with convincingly and, one senses, with enthusiasm! Contrasts of tone have also been handled well; although it is possible that the background could have been made darker and the leaf forms made more distinct, without detracting too much from the strong colour and shapes of the fruit.

contrasts of tone generally handled well – background could have been darker

Texture of the fruit skin rendered convincingly

The oil pastel impasto adds a tactile quality

HELEN The decision to use oil pastels rather than chalk pastels clearly paid off in this drawing. The clarity of strong shapes and the rich impasto of colour lends a tactile quality to the work, which may be lost in reproduction.

The artist decided early on to try to retain the lucidity of the drawing right through to the final stage, and this has meant sacrificing something of the delicacy of the flowers. The fruit has a sumptuousness which is heightened by the dark tone of the background colour.

Dark tone of paper enriches colour values

Garden Scene

DOVECOTE AND FLOWERS

Artists have long been inspired by gardens both formal and informal. Claude Monet, of course, is the supreme example – his garden at Giverny became the source of some of his finest work, including the series of paintings of waterlilies growing beneath a bridge. He realised that he could orchestrate colour using difference species of plants and flowers to create an approximation of preconceived colour schemes.

The subject selected for this project is an old garden attached to an English manor house, now largely destroyed by fire. The dovecote remains intact and its mellow stone provides an interesting contrast to the rich colour and gossamer-like quality of the abundance of flowers in the foreground.

Composition can be critical in dealing with this kind of subject, since you have to try simultaneously to express the dynamism of growth and the solidity of the stonework. Too much concentration on isolated details might lose the sense of actuality and liveliness. Working with pastels, you are less likely to get bogged down with the precise details of individual flower heads and will be able to concentrate instead on treating everything in terms of planes and colour masses. Contrast, too, plays an important part: the intensity of the colour of the flowers is heightened by seeing them against the darker tone of the hedge, for example, and the dovecote is defined by the darker tones of adjacent foliage.

Of course, you are continually having to make adjustments to the colour and tone of a drawing as it progresses from one stage to another. A flat tone which appears dark when first laid, might seem much too light when other colours have been added. The rich, red tone of a flower head might sink into a neutral background tone; whereas a sharply contrasting complementary dark green would make it appear even richer.

Artist · Helen Armstrong

BLACK	BURNT SIENNA	DEEP YELLOW	LIGHT YELLOW	GOLD OCHRE	PRUSSIAN BLUE	BLUE VIOLET	PERMANENT ROSE	MADDER LAKE DEEP

77

1 *The basic composition is drawn sparingly in graphite pencil on a dark ochre sugar paper. White and Cobalt Blue are blended together in the sky.*

2 *The stonework of the buildings is drawn in a light Yellow Ochre and the tone of the paper, which is darker, is allowed to show through in areas of shadow. Prussian Blue is used as an undertone for the foliage.*

3 *More detail is added to the stonework, using a light Yellow Ochre for lighter tones and Olive Green for shadows. Olive Green, Chrome Green Deep and black are fused together on background foliage.*

4 *At this stage, the artist decided that the top half of the drawing had become too detailed. She therefore took the surface pigment off with a tissue, so blurring the details. Greens were then rubbed into the foreground, followed by the sharper linear strokes for stalks and leaves using Olive Green, Chrome Green Light and Chrome Green Deep. A Pthalo Green is also used. The flowerheads are picked out in white, permanent rose, red violet, blue violet, scarlet, Madder Lake Deep and Burnt Sienna.*

5 *A black chalk is now used to bring the drawing together as a single statement, working in tones between stalks in the foreground and adding detail to buildings in the background. Finally, the orange roses are highlighted with Gold Ochre and Burnt Sienna.*

SCARLET	CHROME GREEN DEEP	OLIVE GREEN	CHROME GREEN LIGHT	GREY	COBALT BLUE	YELLOW OCHRE	YELLOW OCHRE TINT

Artist • Cecilia Hunkeler

 78

❶ *An outline drawing of the main shapes is made with a mid-green wax crayon on a sheet of off-white cartridge paper.*

❸ *A stippling technique is used for the flowers using pink, Geranium Red, vermilion, Lemon Yellow, Yellow Ochre and Violet Dark.*

❷ *A mid-grey pastel is worked roughly over the sky and blended with Burnt Sienna and a touch of yellow on the dovecote and other buildings.*

MID GREEN	MID GREY	LEMON YELLOW	YELLOW OCHRE	VERMILION	VIOLET DARK	BURNT SIENNA	BLACK

4 *A thin layer of Permanent Green Light is applied over the whole of the garden area and this is reduced to a transparent tone with a moist sable brush, which allows previous colours to show through.*

5 *More flowers and leaves are stippled in, and the darker recesses of the buildings are drawn in Burnt Sienna blended with black.*

6 *In the final stage, the textural quality of the drawing has been enriched by a combination of scraping out leaf shapes with a steel nib, and by forcing colour through a piece of gauze mesh. The drawing is resolved in terms of colour and tone and without a conspicuous outline.*

Garden Scene • *Critique*

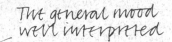

The general mood well interpreted

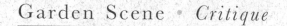

Good use of contrast in terms of texture, colour and tone

HELEN Halfway through this drawing, the artist realised her mistake in developing the top part of the composition at the expense of the rest of the drawing. You should always consider the drawing as a whole and not concentrate too much on one area. In this project, the artist's primary interest in fact lay in the way that the bright colour of the flowers contrasted with the dark tone of the hedge. The early attention to architectural details detracted from this, which is why she wiped the surface pigment away in order to simplify the background. One must always be prepared to spoil things a little in order to gain ground. In this instance, you can see how, in the final stage of the drawing, the artist has managed to resolve the tonal balance of the drawing in a way that draws attention to the garden flowers, rather than focusing on background detail.

SOPHIE The artist herself felt that the choice of such a dark-toned pastel paper was a mistake – although I would disagree, since I feel it allows the richness of colour to become more evident in the final stage of the drawing. I like the general mood, atmosphere and sense of place that comes across in the drawing. The flowers are shown *en masse* without any fussy detail, and this works well in contrast to the solidity of the stone dovecote in the background.

Everything has been resolved in terms of tonal balance

Ar

❶

the n
drav
color

Intelligent combination
of oil and chalk pastels
to give a variety of texture

Perhaps the path
should have been
extended

❸

us
B

CECILIA In this drawing, the artist has gone to considerable
lengths to recreate the textural contrasts of weathered stone and
the delicacy of the flowers, creeper and hedge. Using a combination of oil and chalk pastels, she has worked and reworked some
parts of the drawing in such a way that one has the sense that everything has been rebuilt in her own terms.

Contrasts of colour and tone work without being too boldly
defined. Compositionally, it might have been interesting to extend
the path bordering the flowers in the foreground.

Artist • Cecilia Hunkeler

84

94

❶ *The main outline of the houses is drawn in blue crayon onto a grey-green Canson paper.*

❷ *A rich vermilion is worked into the façade of the house on the left, and the same colour carried through to details on other houses. The basic greens of the tree foliage are drawn in contrasting tones of Olive Green on the left, and a Dark Chrome Green on the right.*

❸ *An off-white tone is worked into the façades of the central house, and the adjacent house on the extreme right. A pale light brown tint provides a halftone in the shadows. More tones are added to the foliage and to the house on the extreme left. Some of the darker recesses of the windows are drawn in charcoal grey.*

DARK
BLUE

COBALT
BLUE

ULTRAMARINE

OLIVE
GREEN

DARK
CHROME
GREEN

VERMILION

ORANGE

PALE
BROWN

GREY

95

4 *Blended tones of ultramarine and Cobalt Blue are added to the sky at full strength and overworked with white chalk for the clouds on the left. The colour of the facade of the red house is modified by working over the vermilion with grey and orange. White chalk is used to restate the window frames and the wooden supports to balconies and canopies.*

5 *All the decorative architectural details under the eaves, windows, porches, stairs and so on, are now added. The weatherboarding is picked up in successive strokes of white, cream and grey. The foliage is more carefully defined and colours in the sky softly blended.*

Artist • Sophie Mason

1 *The main structure of the buildings is drawn directly on white cartridge paper with a pencil and grey crayon.*

2 *A light mauve is selected as a mid-tone to establish the shadows in all the recesses, such as doorways, eaves, balconies and so on.*

3 *Naples Yellow is spread thinly over the buildings to suggest sunlight and to contrast with the cooler lilac hue. The drawing is restated in pencil.*

| NAPLES YELLOW | MARS VIOLET LIGHT | PERMANENT RED LIGHT | PURPLE | CERULEAN BLUE LIGHT | OLIVE GREEN | HOOKER'S GREEN | DARK GREY |

97

4 *The warm tones are intensified with Permanent Red Light. Darker tones of violet are added to shadows and grey to windows and the eaves of the building.*

6 *Cerulean Blue is scumbled into areas of the sky and is also blended with the foliage and on parts of the windows. A grey pastel is used to draw the weatherboard structure of the wooden building. Olive Green is added to the trees.*

5 *Mars Violet Light provides a pale shadow which is blended with other colours. Hooker's Green is loosely drawn into the foliage and some Burnt Umber is added to areas in shadow.*

Artist • Sophie Mason

❶ *A preliminary pencil drawing is made on a cream-coloured cartridge paper, with additional strokes in Burnt Sienna and Yellow Ochre pastel pencils.*

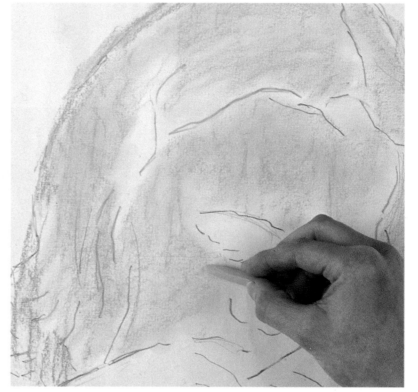

❷ *Using the flat side of a stick of Yellow Ochre, a broad tint is laid and spread with fingers to achieve a base colour for the head.*

❸ *Burnt Umber is used both for the guinea pig and for darker tones on the girl's face.*

VIOLET DARK | NAPLES YELLOW | PALE COBALT BLUE | TURQUOISE | BURNT SIENNA | BURNT UMBER | DARK GREY | CADMIUM RED | YELLOW OCHRE | BLACK

4 *A grey pastel is introduced to indicate very freely the striped pattern of the girl's shirt. Black pastel is smudged over the background to create tonal contrast. A touch of red is added to the mouth.*

5 *Violet Dark is used in short strokes for the hair on the guinea pig and also on the girl's hair. Some drawing is done in pencil to redefine the shape of the girl's face. A green-gold is introduced on the hair as well as touches of Yellow Ochre and Burnt Sienna, using pastel pencils.*

6 *Blues are blended into the background and more black and Raw Umber to provide richness of colour and contrast. More definition is given to the face, and some areas are brought out and highlighted by Naples Yellow. Pale blue is drawn over the grey on the stripes of the shirt.*

Animal Study · *Critique*

A skilful treatment of varied textural qualities

Girls hands are awkwardly placed

HELEN There are a lot of subtleties in this drawing which may not be immediately apparent (or may be lost in reproduction). Notice, for instance, how the artist has managed to convey the softness of the girl's hair and complexion by a careful blending of warm and cool hues of chalk pastels. Notice, too, how a feathering technique has been used to render the modelling of the girl's features. Again, the treatment of the animal has been arrived at by careful analysis of the colour and textures. My only reservation lies in the way that the girl's hands seem awkwardly placed in terms of the overall composition of the drawing.

background tone is too level
in relation to other tones

could have
been more
contrast
in the folds
of the hair

SOPHIE From the outset, the artist made the decision to get as close to the model as possible by focusing on the expressive qualities which are the essence of this subject. All extraneous detail has been eliminated, including the awkwardness of the hands. The artist herself felt uneasy about the over-sentimentality of the subject, but she has nevertheless managed to render the drawing with considerable feeling and sensitivity.

All extraneous detail
has been eliminated

Expressive
qualities
emphasized

CECILIA The overriding sentiment and pathos of the subject has been handled in a sympathetic way. The artist has also successfully employed a variety of pastel techniques to convey the range of textural qualities. The background tone, in my view, is too level in relation to the other tones, and could have been a shade darker. Again, there could have been slightly more contrast when dealing with the folds of the girl's hair.

Artist • Sophie Mason

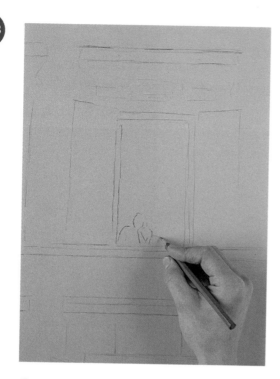

❶ *A warm light brown paper was selected in relation to the overall colour scheme. The main lines of the building – lintels, shutters and window – are drawn in with a Brown Umber pastel pencil.*

❷ *The lightest tone on the stucco is drawn with a Naples Yellow crayon (water-soluble).*

❸ *Yellow Ochre and Raw Sienna are roughly blended with a finger over the main area of the building.*

| CADMIUM YELLOW | NAPLES YELLOW | RAW SIENNA LIGHT | YELLOW OCHRE | RAW SIENNA | VERMILION | BURNT UMBER | BLACK |

4 *The shutters are drawn with Burnt Umber, and the same colour is used for areas of shadow. The dark recess of the window is drawn in black, isolating the figures of the children.*

5 *Some variety is given to the texture of the wall with pale Cadmium Yellow which is blended with colours applied previously. Black and Burnt Umber are used to provide more definition. Touches of Permanent Red Light and ochre are used to highlight the children's faces and arms.*

6 *Vermilion is used on the girl's dress. Most of the work in the final stage is expended on the texture of the wall. The slats of the shutters are carefully drawn using a Violet Dark crayon. Finally, part of the colour is softened with a brush and water.*

Townscape • *Critique*

The freshness
of the early
stages slightly
lost in the
final stage

Balance between
colour, tonal values
and descriptive
detail is successfully
achieved

HELEN The early stages of this project worked well when the colour was softly rubbed in. The freshness of these early stages was slightly lost when architectural detail was superimposed. Nevertheless, the texture of the crumbling stucco has been handled well, and the whole atmosphere of the drawing is strongly evocative of the subject. It is always difficult to get the balance right between colour and tonal values and descriptive detail: the artist has, in the final stage of the drawing, managed to get this about right.

convincing rendering of the surface qualities of decaying stuccos

SOPHIE The overall colour and composition works well in this drawing. The medium has been fully exploited to render the rich and varied texture of the stucco walls. The artist herself has reservations about combining crayons with pastels; there are some subjects, however, which demand unusual combinations of media to achieve the desired effect. Again, although the artist felt that the drawing had been overworked in the final stage, she has, in my view, achieved about the right balance between colour and descriptive drawing.

Good colour and composition

CECILIA The artist has enjoyed the challenge of trying to produce a convincing drawing of the surface qualities of decaying stucco. The scraping technique is particularly effective in this instance, conveying the illusion of recessed patterns in the mouldings above the windows. Chalk and oil pastels have been successfully combined to produce a bas-relief effect.

The drawing of the children is carefully understated in relation to the wealth of surrounding texture. This is a good example of the way that materials can be harnessed to serve the intentions of the artist.

Judicious use of mixed media

Seascape

FISHING JETTY

In the half light of dawn or dusk, the main features in a land-scape are reduced to silhouettes and everything appears to be abstracted to a basic two-dimensional pattern. At sunrise or sunset there is a scattering of light caused by the molecules of air and the presence of dust and moisture in the atmosphere. Because the overall illumination is less intense, and the quality of light more even, the contrast between light and dark areas is much softer. The tonal scale is therefore easier to define.

In this scene of fishermen off the coast of Malaysia, the wooden jetty acts as a visual device which leads the eye from one side of the composition to the other. The continuous horizontal rhythm of the composition is interrupted only by the standing figure of one of the fishermen. It is a subject which calls for restraint and a careful balance between softly-blended nuances of colour and tone, overlaid by a sharply defined silhouette which will hold everything together.

The versatility of the pastel medium becomes more apparent when dealing with subjects such as this, especially when chalk and oil pastels are combined to suggest how sea can appear both opaque and translucent, while still reflecting the hues of the sky.

Artist • Helen Armstrong

| BLACK | PRUSSIAN BLUE | ULTRAMARINE DEEP | ULTRAMARINE TINT | BLUE VIOLET | COBALT BLUE | RED VIOLET DEEP | YELLOW OCHRE TINT |

❶ *The basic outlines of the composition are drawn in pencil on a Fabriano 'duck egg' blue paper.*

❷ *The flat side of a mid-toned blue is wiped across the area of the sky and sea. The pigment is then rubbed with a soft tissue on the sky and reflections on the water.*

❸ *Successive strokes of mauve, cream and white are blended with tissue to lighten the sky. Lighter tints are also added on the smooth sea around the wooden jetty. Prussian Blue is blended into the sea and sky on the lefthand side of the composition. Cobalt Blue suggests reflected light beneath the jetty.*

❹ *The horizon is redefined with Prussian Blue and this is carried through to other parts of the drawing including the land, jetty and boats. Black is worked over the blue on the jetty and the boats and reflections are drawn in ultramarine with a touch of black.*

❺ *The tone of the water in the foreground is made much darker with Cobalt Blue, violet and black. A light blue is overlaid between the jetty posts to suggest waves in the sea. A diminutive spot of mauve picks up the lighthouse light. The black on the jetty is moderated by overdrawing with ultramarine. Coarser strokes are used in the foreground and partially blended with a finger.*

Artist • Cecilia Hunkeler

134

❶ *The structure of the wooden jetty, boats, the headland and clouds are tentatively outlined in a dark blue crayon on a tinted ultramarine Canson paper.*

❷ *Specks of Prussian Blue and Cobalt Blue are stippled on the sea in the foreground. A paler tint of Cobalt Blue is added above the stippled texture and along the horizon. A touch of violet is introduced to the sea below the jetty in the extreme left.*

❸ *A pale mauve tint is blended into the sky on the right and extended to the sea in spaces defined by the structure of the jetty. The same colour is stippled into the sea in the foreground. A darker blue-violet is then drawn into the sky on the left, and immediately reduced to a transparent tint with a wet brush. A pale cobalt tint is also blended into the sea on the left, from the horizon to the jetty.*

| DARK BLUE | COBALT BLUE | PRUSSIAN BLUE | PALE VIOLET | DARK VIOLET | PINK | BLACK |

135

4 *The stippling in the foreground is almost cancelled out by a layer of Cobalt Blue. The undulations of the waves are defined with a dark Prussian Blue. Warm hints of red-violet and mauve are added to the sky. A granular chalky blue is laid over part of the white chalk in the top lefthand side of the composition.*

5 *White and pink chalks are blended in the sky in the top half of the composition and then softened with a wet brush. The headland and boats are filled in with black chalk, and a richer oil pastel pigment of Cobalt Blue added to the sea on the right below the jetty.*

6 *The figures standing on the jetty and the structure itself are drawn in black oil pastel. The reflections of the structure are added in the same tone. The waves in the foreground are treated with a variety of textures, including stippling and scraping. The sky from the horizon to the clouds is blended to a softer tone. Finally, more work is done on the clouds, and to enhance the reflected pattern of light on the sea.*

Artist • Sophie Mason

136 **❶** *The grey-blue Ingres paper was selected in relation to the overall colour bias of the subject. The outlines of the jetty in the foreground are drawn with Burnt Umber and Raw Umber pastel pencils. The clouds are suggested with a few pencil strokes.*

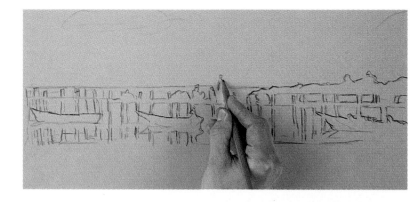

❷ *The foreground is roughed in using a Prussian Blue pastel (used on its side). The main structure of the jetty is drawn in Burnt Umber.*

❸ *Cobalt Blue and Dark Cobalt Blue are blended together to suggest the mass of sky above the low horizon.*

NAPLES YELLOW	PERMANENT RED LIGHT	VIOLET LIGHT	COBALT BLUE	DARK BLUE	PRUSSIAN BLUE	BURNT UMBER	RAW UMBER	BLACK

137

4 *A tint of Permanent Red Light is used to lend emphasis to the shapes of the boats and around the structure of the jetty. A tint of pink is added to the sky, producing a contrast between warm and cool hues.*

5 *Short strokes of violet are introduced to the sky near the horizon. Naples Yellow is used to lighten certain areas in the picture, and more Cobalt Blue is added to water and sky.*

6 *The depth and detail are brought to the fore using ultramarine and Prussian Blue pastel pencils. Burnt Umber and black pencils are also used to darken some areas and to intensify the tones of boats and fishermen. Finally, more Permanent Red Light and violet are blended into the sky.*

Fishing Scene · *Critique*

Sky and sea handled well in terms of the medium

HELEN The treatment of the sky and water has been executed with considerable skill and with an astute awareness of the capabilities of the medium. Silhouettes are notoriously difficult to deal with: if, on the one hand, they are too sharply defined, they become too conspicuous; if they are rendered too softly, the identity of the shape is lost. In this drawing, I feel that the artist might have used another medium for the silhouette of the wooden jetty – ink, perhaps, or gouache applied with a fine brush.

Perhaps a different medium for the drawing of the jetty would have been better

Good feeling for light and atmosphere

SOPHIE The artist has deliberately set the horizon line low in the composition in order to concentrate on the sky. The blending of warm and cool hues, and the descriptive, free-ranging strokes help to invest the drawing with interest.

The jetty itself is perhaps too brown and could have been darker in tone, but the overall feeling for light and atmosphere is convincing and handled well in terms of the medium.

The jetty could have been darker in tone

The prevailing mood of the subject has been captured well —

The silhouette of the jetty is slightly too conspicuous

CECILIA The pervading mood of this subject has been captured very well in this drawing, particularly in the way that the light has been controlled. Additionally, the artist has managed to suggest the translucent nature of water convincingly by combining chalk and oil pastels, and then by burnishing, scraping, stippling and reworking the surface. I particularly like the symbolic quality of the drawing of the upper part of the sky.

The silhouette of the jetty, boats and figures are perhaps a fraction too conspicuous – this might have been resolved by blending in a touch of indigo or Prussian Blue.

Glossary

A

AERIAL PERSPECTIVE

Also called atmospheric perspective; relates to the suggested recession in landscape subjects achieved by taking account of the fact that tones appear to be reduced by atmosphere as they recede towards the distance.

B

BINDER

The ingredient used in the manufacture of paints and pastels to hold the materials together and help them adhere to paper, board or canvas.

BLENDING

Merging or fusing together two or more colours using a brush, torchon or your finger.

BODY COLOUR

An opaque paint such as gouache or watercolour which has been mixed with opaque white gouache.

BURNISH

(a) To rub colours together with your fingers or a torchon to produce a glossy surface lustre; (b) To take an impression from a woodblock, linotype or monotype by continuous rotational rubbing movements with a spoon or brayer (special burnishing tool) on the back of printing paper.

C

CHARCOAL

Sticks of charred willow or vine used as a drawing medium.

COLOUR WHEEL

Twelve distinct colours - primary, secondary and tertiary - arranged in equal progression around a circle.

COMPLEMENTARY COLOURS

Complementary colours are found opposite each other on the colour wheel. A colour is complementary to the one with which it contrasts must strongly, such as red with green.

COMPOSITION

The satisfactory disposition of all the related elements in a drawing or painting.

CONTÉ

A very hard crayon named after the eighteenth century scientist who invented it Nicholas-Joseph Conté (1755–1805).

E

ESSENCE

An essential oil extracted from plants or animal substances; an example is lavender oil, which can be used as a solvent for oil paints and oil pastels.

F

FEATHERING

A pastel technique which involves using light, rapid strokes which have a kinetic effect on the drawing, imbuing it with a sense of movement.

FILLER

Usually white pigment which is added to paints and pastels to extend the range of coloured tints.

FIXATIVE

A thin, transparent varnish sprayed onto the surface of a drawing (in pencil, charcoal or chalk pastel) to make it stable, that is, to stop the pigment from falling off the support. It also prevents smudging.

FORM

The three-dimensional appearance of a shape in drawing or painting.

FUGITIVE

A term used to
describe colours that
are liable to fade
under strong light or
in the course of time.

G

GOUACHE

An opaque form of
watercolour combining
coloured pigments and
white filler and bound
in gum. See body
colour.

GROUND

The first colour laid
on the surface as a
preliminary tone.

GUM ARABIC

In its purest form,
the sap produced by
acacia trees; used
as a binding medium
in pastels and
watercolours.

H

HUE

The colour, rather
than the tone, of a pig-
ment or object.

I

IMPASTO

A heavy, paste-like application of paint
or oil pastel which produces a dominant
texture.

L

LOCAL COLOUR

The actual colour of an object, such as the
red of an apple, rather than the colour the
object appears when it is modified by light
or shadow.

M

MEDIUM

(a) The type of material used to produce a
drawing or painting, e.g. charcoal, pastel,
watercolour, oil etc; (b) a substance blended
with paint to thicken, thin or dry the paint.

MERGING

The blending of two or more colours gradually so that there are subtle gradations from
one hue to another without conspicuous
seams or joins.

MODELLING

Expressing the volume and solidity of an
object by light and shade.

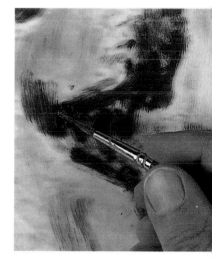

142

MONOCHROME

A painting or drawing produced using single colour, gradations of colour, or in black and white.

MONOTYPE

A single print made by painting with oil paint or printer's ink onto a slab of glass and then transferring the image to paper by burnishing it from the back.

P

PALETTE

The range of colours selected individually by the artist; also refers to the surface on which colours are mixed.

PERSPECTIVE

A means of creating the illusion of three-dimensions when drawing or painting on a two-dimensional surface. Linear perspective makes use of parallel lines which converge on a vanishing point. Aerial perspective suggests distance by the use of tone.

PIGMENT

The coloured matter of paint or pastels originally derived from plants, animal, vegetable and mineral products; generally synthesized chemically in paint manufacture.

S

SCUMBLE

To work a layer of opaque paint or pastel over an existing colour in such a way that

the colour of the layer beneath is seen through the broken texture of the top layer.

SGRAFFITO

A technique used in oil pastel when the design is scratched through the top layer of colour to reveal the lower layer.

STIPPLING

A technique of shading in pastel drawing using closely spaced dots or flecks of colour.

T

TINT

A colour that is lighter in tone than its primary or parent colour; usually obtained by adding white or a diluting agent.

TONE

The light and dark value of a colour; for example, pale red is the same tone as pale ochre but both are lighter in tone than dark brown.

TOOTH

The degree of roughness caused by the raised texture of certain drawing papers, which enables the pastel or charcoal to adhere to the surface.

TORCHON

(Also tortillon or paper stump) A tightly furled stick of soft paper used for blending chalk pastels, pencil, conté and charcoal.

WASH

Dilute colour applied to paper to produce an evenly spread thin transparent film.

Index

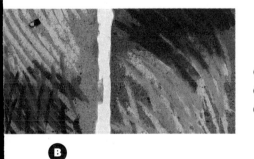

Index